Thank You Body, Thank You Heart

A Gratitude and Self-Compassion Practice for Bedtime

Jennifer Cohen Harper

Illustrated by Karen Gilmour

Thank You Body, Thank You Heart
Copyright © 2019 Jennifer Cohen Harper

Published by:
PESI Publishing & Media
PESI, Inc.
3839 White Ave.
Eau Claire, WI 54703

Illustrations: Karen Gilmour
Cover: Karen Gilmour & Amy Rubenzer
ISBN: 9781683732600

Library of Congress Control Number:2019948977

PESI
Publishing
& Media
www.pesipublishing.com

For Isabelle and Hazel.
With gratitude and awe. - JCH

To the Alluem Kids.
Thank you for your presence.
Thank you for your beautiful hearts. - KG

Welcome Letter

YOU are IMPORTANT. Welcome to this journey of
gratitude and self-compassion. Yes, I'm talking about
this book, but hopefully also about your life!

You may be a parent, teacher, guardian, friend, sibling,
or maybe you are reading this book to yourself. No matter
who you are, your unique body, mind and heart have a role
to play in making this world a loving and healthy place for
children everywhere.

Each and every person is an irreplaceable marvel.
Did you forget to be in awe of yourself today?
I probably did too. I'm so glad that you are here now,
so we can remember together.

Much love,

  Jenn

Thank you feet that
worked all day.

You helped me stand,
you helped me play.

Thank you legs that
are so strong.

You moved and grooved
me right along.

Feet and legs, now
you can rest.

All day you did
your very best.

Belly, you deserve some praise.

You keep me healthy in many ways.

Take a break and while I sleep,
get ready for tomorrow's food to eat.

Back that kept me sitting tall,
you rarely get a break at all.

You twist and turn and lift
and bend, but now the day
is at an end.

Chest and lungs that let me breathe, you work and work without reprieve.

Caring for me in dark and light, I'm grateful for your work tonight.

Thank you heart for beating steady.

Whether I'm nervous or brave,
you're always ready.

Supporting me in all I do,
I'm strong and proud
because of you.

Arms and shoulders,
you've held the load
of all I've carried, pulled
and thrown.

Your muscles may
feel pretty sore,
but tonight you
won't work any more.

Hands I want to give you a high five for all the patient work you've tried.

Drawing, cutting, carrying stuff, does all that doing ever get tough?

Neck you are
so very strong.

You hold my head
up all day long.

Turning left and
turning right,
now you're done
for the night.

Thank you eyes
for guiding me
through a world that
has so much to see.

I'll look for beauty
all around,
but tonight let's just
sleep safe and sound.

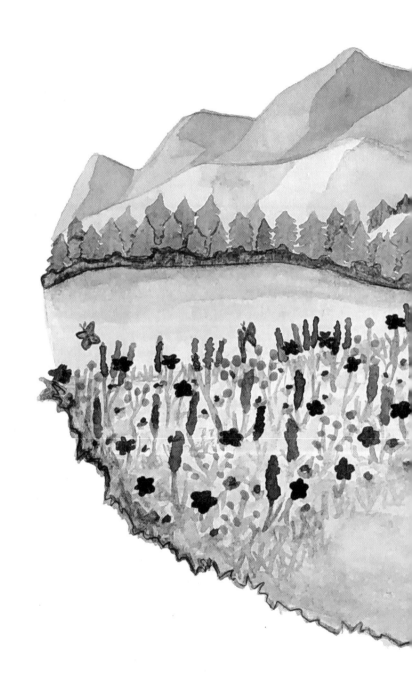

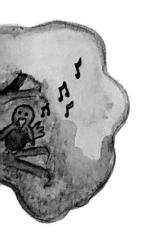

Birds and friends
and lullabies.

Ears that listen
are a prize.

Sometimes quiet
can be nice too.

I hope it feels
as good for you.

Nose, you bring me yummy scents, like pie and flowers and peppermints.

But sometimes you protect me too.

Thank you nose for all you do.

I'm grateful for a mind that knows I'm special from my head to toes.

And that all of me deserves to rest, so all of me can do my best.

Tomorrow I'll be on my way,
ready to start a brand new day.

But tonight I'll give some loving care
to this body that takes me everywhere.

 Thank you feet and legs

 Thank you chest and lungs

 Thank you belly

 Thank you heart

 Thank you back

 Thank you arms

 Thank you
hands

 Thank you
nose

 Thank you
eyes

 Thank you
mind

 Thank you
ears

 Thank you
body

Tomorrow I'll be on my way,
ready to start a brand new day.
But tonight I'll give some loving care
to this body that takes me everywhere.

Note to Caregivers

Thank you for taking the time to explore gratitude and self-compassion with the children in your life.

There are many things that will shape a child's relationship with their own body. Many of them are outside of our control, but the more we can do to create a healthy identity early on, the more resilient our kids will be when faced with wildly competing messages about their worth.

One consideration is that often, as our kids get older, they relate more and more to their body based on the way it looks. Actually, I find the world already relates to my young daughters based on how they look! If we can remember to help kids orient to their body in terms of function and feeling, we can help them become more embodied people, with better self-awareness, and an increased ability to understand and meet their own needs.

You can make this book a regular part of your nighttime ritual, but if your children want other stories or they start to move away from it as they get older, the short body-scan content on the prior pages offers an easy guide to keep the practice a consistent part of your routine.

I hope that you, and the children in your life, fall more in love with yourselves each day.

With love and gratitude,

Jenn

Author & Illustrator

Jennifer Cohen Harper is an educator, author, public speaker and mother, who works to support all children and teens in the development of strong inner resources through the tools of yoga and mindfulness. Her goal is to help kids, and those who care for them, thrive in the world regardless of circumstances, and navigate the many challenges they face with a sense of personal power and self-awareness. Jenn is the founder and CEO of Little Flower Yoga + Mindfulness.

Karen Gilmour has been drawing, painting, coloring and creating for as long as she can remember. Her art has been seen in books, on back to school supplies and on the walls of classrooms and kid's rooms. When Karen isn't creating art, she is busy as the director of Alluem Kids, an ever growing yoga program for kids, teens and families at Alluem Yoga in Cranford, NJ. You can see more of Karen's work by visiting: www.karengilmour.com.